Table of Contents

List of Figures

List of Tables

I. Overview

This is the final report on the Information Survivability project at the MIT Artificial Intelligence Laboratory. The work was conducted in the period January 1,1998 through December 31, 1999. The project aimed to exploit representations and techniques used in AI research and development to support the construction of Survivable Information Services.

The central premise of this work is that a significant shift of focus and approach is necessary in order to deal with the emerging threat of information attacks on the critical infrastructures of our society. A range of studies, for example those conducted by the RAND Corporation and by a DARPA ISAT project, raised the concern that a concerted information attack by a skillful and motivated opponent could lead to catastrophic consequences. In particular, it was observed that the increasingly reliance by the Department of Defense on advanced information technologies made it particularly vulnerable to such attacks. Information attacks have few physical warning signs, are often extremely difficult to detect, are difficult to distinguish from normal malfunctions, and are capable of interfering with or totally disabling complex military operations. Finally, it was observed that traditional security techniques only address part of the problem; they attempt to prevent attacks, but they offer little once an attack has been successfully launched.

The approach adopted by the MIT research team was to assume that attacks could be successfully launched. The evidence for this seemed overwhelming: Red teams have been able to penetrate virtually all systems tested in relatively short order. Secondly, traditional security techniques are aimed at keeping out attackers, but tend to ignore the possibility of a compromised insider. Thus, instead of trying to build impenetrable and secure systems, the research group adopted the approach of detecting attacks and attempting to reconfigure the information systems involved to insure the survivability and sustainability of the critical services being provided.

The following imaginary scenario illustrates the types of subtle attacks that are believed to be realistic. The scenario illustrates the ability of an attack to interfere with military operations; it also illustrates the "stealthy" nature of such attacks. Unlike physical attacks, information attacks have no major associated event involving the physical presence of the attacker. In fact, it is often difficult to ascertain whether an attack has actually transpired. Finally, even if it is clear that an attack has happened it is still often impossible to infer the intentions of the attackers.

II. A Scenario

It was late Sunday evening, July 16, 2006 when the first alarm indicators began to appear at the headquarters of the US 101st Fighter Wing at their base in Saudi Arabia. The flight planning system was going through its usual paces, planning the next set of routine missions over Iraq's no-fly zone, when the diagnostic system reported that the planning was taking too long.

Diagnostic software went into action to determine the source of the problem and what to do about it. Working from its description of the overall structure and behavior of the system (an electronic version of the system block diagram and other documentation), the diagnostic software determined that mission planning required information from ground-based intelligence supplied by CIA, aerial photo reconnaissance from NRO, mission focus information from the Joint Chiefs, and aircraft readiness information from the logistics systems. Monitoring and measurements indicated that all but the last of these seemed to be performing up to specs; only the logistics information was slow in coming.

The diagnostic software then ``dug down'' into the documentation for the logistics system, determined that it was in turn composed of 3 systems handling information about individual aircraft status, supplies availability, and pilot availability. Of these three the last appeared to be growing increasingly slow in its response time.

Another reference to the system documentation indicated that the pilot availability system was in fact a distributed application currently running at three sites in Europe. At this point the system began further probes, this time directed at those particular physical installations, which indicated that one of the three sites providing the pilot availability function was currently the target of a storm of network requests, clearly intended to produce a denial of service as the machine attempted to keep up with the requests. The diagnostic system sent off email warnings to the appropriate people and programs at both the site in Europe and at the DoD's NIH (Network Institute of Health), warning about the attack.

Selecting an appropriate subset of DoD systems, it then sent out a broadcast message announcing the need for a system to provide part of the pilot availability service. Within a few seconds it had received several bids to take on the task from among those systems, with each bid indicating what resources the responding machine could apply to the task, likely response times, etc. Choosing the best of these, it informed the other two sites in Europe that part of the pilot availability task was being taken over by a new location, and noted that soon thereafter the speed of the no-fly zone mission planning was back up to normal.

III. Implications of the Scenario: Approaches to Intrusion Detection

The scenario illustrates the several key problems that must be addressed. What are observable are **symptoms,** behaviors of the computation other than those intended. What one wants to know, on the other hand, is what's wrong? Has there been an attack? If so, what kind of attack? What resources has it affected? How has it affected those resources? Can those resources be trusted for future computations? If not, how should the computations be carried out?

Several approaches to intrusion detection have already been developed. They all make different tradeoffs between the dual problems of false-positives and false-negatives. We will first describe the causes of these problems, outline the structure of the space of intrusion detection systems and then explain where our approach fits into this space and how it represents a fundamentally new approach that is not as prone to these problems.

The earliest intrusion detection systems were built around a library of known attacks. These systems attempt to match the current data to this library. When an attack is recognized, these techniques are quite informative; they know exactly what type of attack has been launched and can therefore predict with some certainty what resources might have been compromised as a result. False negatives arise when the system is knowledge-poor, in particular when its library of known attacks does not include the actual attack. In effect, this class of systems is the class of *Expert systems* for intrusion detection; it is subject to the classic brittleness of expert systems, when the problem falls off the "knowledge cliff" the system fails with a false negative.

In an attempt to counteract these shortcomings, a different type of system was developed. Instead of recognizing specific attacks, these systems rather built a statistical profile of normal user behavior and then looked for behavior that did not match this profile. Since there is no reliance on a catalog of attacks, there is no problem with the incompleteness of the library. However, there are dual problems. First of all, when such a system does detect a deviation from the statistical profile it is usually quite uninformative about what is wrong; at best, it can say that the user (or process) is behaving outside its normal range. It is unclear what kind of attack this might indicate or whether it indicates an attack at all. In fact, such systems in practice have exhibited a very high false positive rate, identifying benign user behavior as an attack because it somehow false outside the range of normal. Thus, this class of system is that class of *anomaly detectors*, sharing the usual problems of anomaly detector systems: false positives and a failure to provide precise characterizations of the problem.

The third class of systems attempts to avoid the problems of the above methods using *machine learning*. These systems are trained against a corpus of labeled data including attacks and normal behavior. The machine learning algorithms attempt to generalize the attack data producing a recognizer capable of identifying all the attacks in the training set as well as others not present in the data. However, these systems are still limited by the data: attacks dissimilar to the training data are not recognized and normal behavior dissimilar to the benign behaviors in the training set may be labeled as attacks by some of the algorithms. In practice, the machine learning intrusion detectors represent a compromise between the first two categories; they produce fewer false negatives than the expert system intrusion detectors (although their scope is dependent on the training data and they do still have a knowledge cliff) and they produce fewer false positives than the anomaly detectors since they will only alarm when the data resembles training data that has been labeled as an attack.

There is a simple 2 by 2 matrix that helps to understand the sources of the strengths and weaknesses of these approaches. On one dimension we divide systems based on whether they are driven by statistical profiles or models of structure and function. On the other dimension we divide systems by whether they attempt to directly recognize bad behavior or instead attempt to notice deviations from expected or normal behavior. Anomaly detectors are driven by statistical profiles and notice deviations from normal. In the diagonally opposite quadrant are the expert systems, driven by models and direct recognition of malign behavior. It is therefore not surprising that these two classes of systems have directly complementary problems: One suffers from false positives because its statistical profile is under informed about normal behavior and it is driven by detecting deviations; the other suffers from false negatives because its catalog of attack models is under informed about the breadth of attacks and it is driven by matching the data to an existing model. Machine learning systems represent a compromise; they occupy a common row or column with each of the other categories.

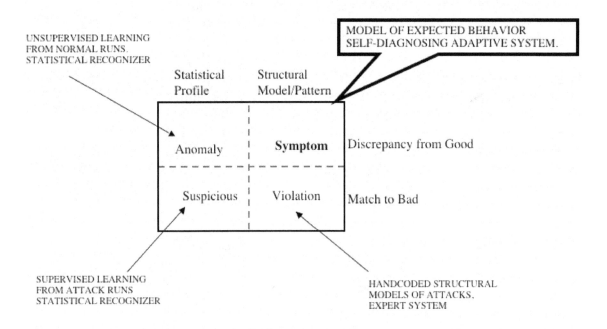

Figure 1: The space of intrusion detection systems

Our work occupies the fourth quadrant. It is driven by a model of the system's intended behavior; it works by recognizing deviations from this model. Such an approach is not subject to false negatives, because any deviation from the expected behavior will be

4

noticed as abnormal. It is informative, characterizing precisely how the behavior deviates from the normal. As we will show later, one can make strong statistical inferences about the nature of the attacks that might have caused the misbehavior. The approach is also not prone to false positives since the behavior model precisely characterizes correct or intended behavior. Thus, we believe that this *model-based diagnosis* approach represents both a fundamentally new approach as well as one that make complementary and better tradeoffs.

IV. Scope of the work

The work originally proposed to DARPA involved a thorough investigation into the above set of questions. The approach represented a significant change of focus: rather than attempting to prevent attacks by constructing provably secure systems, the proposed research instead shifted to the question of responding to and surviving attacks. This leads to several new questions as the core of the research:

- How do we describe attacks? What framework and vocabulary enable one to deal with the huge variety of exploits that are already know about and more importantly how does one deal with the seemingly ever increasing body of new exploits that hackers employ?

- What techniques can be employed to detect attacks? Hackers routinely develop new techniques for attacking systems and every new release of a complex software system seems to create new opportunities for information attacks. For every key exploit, there are a large number of variations. Thus merely cataloging attack seems to be a hopeless pursuit. What other approaches are possible? What kinds of reasoning or pattern matching techniques might be appropriate?

- What should a system do once an attack is noticed? Not all attacks have the same consequences and not all attacks affect all machines in the same way. How can a computation reconfigure itself to capitalize on the existence of resources that are uncompromised or at least are less compromised than others?

The proposed work involved several tasks each aimed at providing technology relevant to different parts of the problem outlined above. The proposed statement of work was for three years. However, DARPA elected to fund a subset of the proposed tasks over a shorter period of time. In particular, the funded project involved the following three tasks

A. Task 1: Developing an ontology of information attacks

We will begin our work by reviewing the years of experience that have been had with attacks on computer networks, with an eye to organizing it to provide a sense of the range of phenomena that will need to be considered. One recent source of identifies three very general kinds of attacks: intrusions, denial of service, and information theft. Beneath this there is considerably more detail, including viruses, Trojan horses, spoofing of various sorts, etc. The product of the work will be a draft ontology that will be updated continuously as the work progresses; success will be measured by its ability to provide a foundation in designing a behavior description language for the model-based reasoner.

B. Task 2: Build representations of structure and behavior

We will build representations of structure and behavior capable of describing large scale distributed information systems. The structure representation will need to describe both the logical /functional and physical structure of the systems. The logical/functional structure indicates the decomposition of the system by capability, for example a logistics system might be decomposed into three sub-systems dealing with aircraft status, supplies and pilot availability respectively. The physical structure of the systems indicates where each of these components actually resides, for instance the supplies a system was a distributed system running on three specific hosts. Both of these descriptions are necessary for the task, the functional decomposition allows us to focus diagnostic attention on appropriate sub-components; the physical decomposition is important because physical adjacency of malfunctioning components can be a clue as to the nature of the fault.

We will also construct a representation for behavior capable of describing what the system does at each level of physical and functional decomposition. This provides the foundation for prediction of expected behavior, one core of model-based reasoning.

These representations will be constructed on the base of technology provided by our previous work in creating representations and languages for the model-based reasoning task.

C. Task 3: Develop a model based reasoning engine

We will start from existing technology to create a model-based reasoning engine capable of working from the structure and behavior descriptions noted above, predicting expected behavior, comparing it against observations, and using any discrepancies between these two to drive and focus the diagnostic process. While a variety of such engines have been created, there are a number of important differences presented by this task. Chief among them is the notably more difficult task of determining when a discrepancy has occurred. In the world of digital circuits, where most of this work was done, a discrepancy is any difference at all between predictions and observations. Clearly this will be inadequate in this domain where we require a far more sophisticated notion of what differences are significant enough to be worth investigating.

These three tasks focused the effort on the diagnostic task alone, leaving questions of reconfiguration and resource allocation to future work. During the course of the effort, however, we did engage in some activities related to these later questions at DARPA's request. These involved talks given by Dr. Howard Shrobe, Principal Investigator of the project, at a variety of venues including both DARPA meetings other public forums.

V. Summary of Research Results

The key results of the research project can be summarized as follows:

Ontology: It is necessary to describe attacks at multiple levels. At the highest level we describe the useful computational properties that an information system provides to its clients (e.g. data integrity). At the next tier, we describe the computational resources in the domain and their forms of compromise (e.g. the schedule has been compromised to starve out a particular user). At the lowest tier, we describe the vulnerabilities of the computational resources (e.g. susceptibility to buffer overflows) and the set of actions that can exploit the vulnerability. Thus an attack is described as an action that exploits vulnerability in order to compromise a resource and thereby adversely affect a useful property that the system delivers to its users.

Descriptions of structure and functions: Computer systems need to be described at multiple levels in order to reason about the possibility of attacks. At the highest level we decompose a computation into components, connected by data flow and control flow. Each component is described by pre- and post-conditions. The descriptions combine many different aspects of the computation including both functional properties (what is the system supposed to do) and Quality of Service properties (how fast should it do it, with what throughput and latency, etc.) Components of the computation are recursively decomposed to a convenient depth of description. Secondly, the components of the computation should be described in terms of multiple modes of behavior including the expected behavior (the normal mode), known failure modes and a final mode representing any other behaviors not enumerated in the first two categories. Third, the information system should be described in terms of the resources (computers, networks, etc.) used to effect the computation. Each resource similarly has multiple modes of behavior. The behavioral modes of the computational elements are then linked to those of the resources employed.

Reasoning Techniques: There are several techniques for detecting intrusions and attacks. Several of these were developed prior to this project. However, none of these approaches were found to be satisfactory, either because they lack precision or robustness. We discuss this in detail later. The answer developed in this project was to focus on the expected (correct) behavior of the system and to notice deviations from this expected behavior. Any such discrepancy is symptomatic of a compromise due to a successful attack. This approach is preferred because it both provides precise descriptions of the causes of the observed symptom and because it does not rely on pattern matching against a library of known attacks.

Reasoning about attacks should be done using a hybrid of Bayesian and model-based diagnosis techniques. The model-based techniques conduct symbolic deductive reasoning linking the observed symptoms to possible compromised states of the computational resources while the Bayesian techniques associate a degree of certainty with each compromised state that is consistent with the observed symptoms.

VI. Detailed Description of Results[1]

Our premise is that to protect critical computational infrastructures we need to restructure these software systems as *Adaptive Survivable Systems*. In particular, we believe that a software system must be capable of detecting its own malfunction and it must be capable of repairing itself. But this means that it must first be able to *diagnose* the form of the failure; in particular, it must both localize and characterize the breakdown. Our work is set in a difficult context, one in which it is assumed that there is a concerted and coordinated attack by a determined adversary. This context places an extra burden on the diagnostic component of the system. It is no longer adequate merely to determine that a computation has failed to achieve its goal, in addition we wish to determine whether that failure is indicative of a compromise to the underlying infrastructure and whether that compromise is likely to lead to failures of other computations at other times. This research project focuses on the diagnostic component of self adaptivity.

A. Contributions of this Work

We build on previous work in Model-Based diagnosis [1, 3,4,5]. However, the context of our research is significantly different from that of the prior research, leading us to confront several important issues that have not previously been addressed. In particular, we present several new advances in representation and reasoning techniques for model-based diagnosis:

- We develop representation and reasoning techniques for describing and reasoning about the behaviors and failures of *software* systems.

- We develop a new mixed symbolic and Bayesian reasoning technique for model-based diagnosis. The statistical component of the technique utilizes Bayesian networks to calculate accurate posterior probabilities.

- We develop a new heuristic method for finding the most likely diagnosis that utilizes the statistical inferences of the Bayesian network to guide the search.

- We develop techniques for reasoning about common-mode failures. A common-mode failure occurs when the probabilities of the failure modes of two or more components are not independent. This issue has not been previously addressed in the literature on model-based diagnosis.

- We develop techniques for reasoning about intermittent failures.

These are crucial issues when failure is caused by a concerted attack by a malicious opponent. There are many modes of attack but the most pernicious attackers seek to

---

[1] This section is adapted from a papers published in DISCEX and submitted the AAAI National Conference on Artificial Intelligence. It presents the details and results of the research conducted in the project.

avoid detection; therefore they attempt to scaffold the attack slowly, at a nearly undetectable rate. These scaffolding actions will appear as faults (i.e. they will cause the system to behave outside its normal range), but skillful attackers will space them out, making them appear to be highly intermittent. Attackers aim at high leverage points of the infrastructure, such as operating systems or middle-ware. This leads to common-mode faults; because once the operating system has been compromised all application components can be caused to fail at once. The report first reviews the current state of the art in model-based diagnosis; this work has mainly been concerned with breakdowns caused by deterioration of hardware components. In particular, we adopt the framework in [4] where each component has models for each of several behavioral modes and each model is given a probability. Next we turn the question of how to apply these techniques to the diagnosis of complex software systems. Then we extend our modeling framework to account for the fact that software systems are built in layers of infrastructure, with compromises to one layer affecting all higher levels. We present mixed symbolic and statistical diagnostic algorithms for assessing the posterior probabilities of the various behavior modes of each component in the model. As a by-product we develop a heuristic for finding the most likely diagnosis. We present an implementation and show an example of the reasoning process. Finally, we discuss the demands placed on the diagnostic component by our goal of self-adaptivity and conclude with suggestions for future research.

B. Related Research

Model-Based Diagnosis is a symptom directed technique; it is driven by the detection of discrepancies between the observations of actual behavior and the predictions of a model of the system. Almost all of the reported work in the area [1,2,3,4,5] has been concerned with the diagnosis of physical systems subject to routine breakdown. Model-based diagnostic systems use simulation models that compute expected outputs given known inputs; they utilize dependency directed techniques to link each intermediate and final value to the selected behavioral model of any component of the system which was involved in producing that value. The completeness of the diagnostic process is dependent on having bi-directional simulation models for each component of the system. Such models produce both a set of assertions recording what values are expected where and a dependency network linking these assertions to one another and to assertions stating which components must be in a particular behavioral mode for those values to appear. Our work builds on the framework in Sherlock [4] In that work the description of a component includes multiple simulation models, one for each behavioral mode of the component. One distinguished mode is the normal mode, but behavioral models for known failure modes may also be provided. It is also typical to include a null model to account for unknown modes of behavior. Finally, each of the behavioral modes of a component is assigned an *a priori* probability. Sherlock uses these to guide a best first search for a set of behavioral modes, one for each component, such that the models for those modes predict the observed behavior. This is the most likely diagnosis. Sherlock assumed that accurate probabilistic reasoning would be intractable and so approximate techniques were developed. At the time of this work, efficient techniques for Bayesian networks were not yet available.

Because our focus is on detecting the intentional compromise of software components we are forced to face a number of new issues. These include:

- How to model software components in the spirit of model-based diagnosis.

- How to deal with the fact that a compromise to the computational infrastructure (e.g. the operating system) can manifest itself in the malfunction of many application components.

- How to deal with the fact that malfunctions may be intermittent.

- How to reason about the system so as to extract as much information about possible compromises as we can. In particular, we deal with how to use both symbolic and Bayesian techniques.

C. Modeling Software Computations

Model-Based Diagnosis requires completely invertible models of the components in order to guarantee completeness of its analysis. But the components of a complex software system rarely have input-output relationships that are invertible. We therefore look for additional properties that lead to more complete coverage. In particular, we concentrate here on descriptions of computational delay (or other *Quality Of Service* metrics).

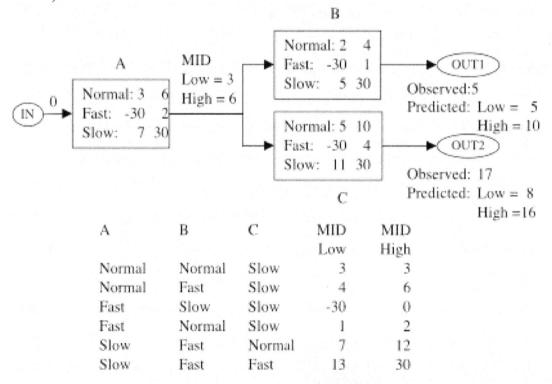

Figure 2: Reasoning About Delay

12

In our current implementation we use an interval of expected delay times (i.e. the computation should run no slower than x and no faster than y) as the behavioral models. Figure 2 shows the application of such models in a framework similar to Sherlock. When propagating in the forward direction we add the delay interval predicted by the behavioral model to the interval bounding the arrival time of the latest input. In the backward direction, we use interval subtraction (and only update the bounds on the last input to arrive). When more than one component predicts the bounds for a particular value (e.g. when a model for component A and a model for component C both predict bounds for the value labeled MID), we take the intersection of the two intervals to obtain the tightest bounds implied by the overall model. A discrepancy is detected when the lower bound of an interval exceeds the upper bound. As in Sherlock we provide several behavioral models for each component, one characterizing normal behavior, others characterizing known failure modes and a null model to cover all other unexpected behaviors. Notice that in Figure 2, there are six potential diagnoses, only one of which involves a single point of failure (in component C). The others involve multiple failures with one component running slower than expected and other components masking the fault at Out1 by running faster than expected. In the third diagnosis, component A runs in ``negative time''! On the surface, such a diagnosis seems physically impossible and we might expect the diagnostic algorithm to reject it. But, the diagnosis algorithm is guided by our representational choices; the reason this diagnosis involves negative time is that the fast behavioral model of component A predicts a delay interval from -30 to +2. The use of a priori probabilities as in Sherlock, can make this diagnosis an unlikely one, but should it?

Suppose that both computations A and C are running on the same computer and further suppose that an attacker had compromised the computer. Under these circumstances, it's not impossible for component C to be delayed (because of a parasitic task inserted by the attacker) while component A has been accelerated, running in less than zero time because it has been hacked by the attacker to send out reasonable answers before it receives its inputs.

What we are able to observe is the progress of a computation; but the computation is itself just an abstraction. What an attacker can actually affect is something physical: the file representing the stored version of a program, the bits in main memory representing the running program, or other programs (such as the operating system) whose services are employed by the monitored application.

D. Common Mode Failures

A single compromise of an operating system component, such as the scheduler, can lead to anomalous behavior in several application components. This is an example of a *common mode failure*; intuitively, a common mode failure occurs when a single fault (e.g. an inaccurate power supply), leads to faults at several observable points in the systems (e.g. several transistors misbehave because their biasing power is incorrect). Another example comes from reliability studies of nuclear power plants where it was observed that the catastrophic failure of a turbine blade could sever several pipes as it flies off, leading to multiple cooling fluid leaks. Formally, there is a common mode failure whenever the probabilities of the failure modes of two (or more) components are dependent. Previous model-based diagnostic systems have assumed probabilistic independence of the behavior modes of different components [4] in order to simplify the assessment of posterior probabilities.

Dealing with common mode failures requires extensions to the modeling framework to make explicit the mechanisms that couple the failure probabilities of different components.

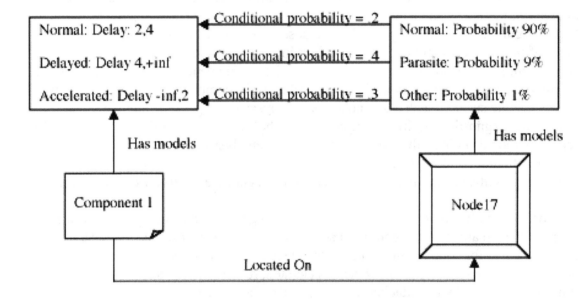

Figure 3: Modeling Computational and Infrastructural Components

We therefore extended our modeling framework, as shown in Figure 3, to include two kinds of objects: computational components (represented by a set of delay models one for each behavioral mode) and infrastructural components (represented by a set of modes, but no delay or other behavioral models). Connecting these two kinds of models are conditional probability links; each such link states how likely a particular behavioral mode of a computational component would be if the infrastructural component that supports that component were in a particular one of its modes. Each infrastructural component mode will usually project conditional probability links to more than one computational component behavioral mode, allowing us to say that normal behavior has some probability of being exhibited even if the infrastructural component has been compromised (however, for simplicity, Figure 3 shows only a one-to-one mapping). The model also includes *a priori* probabilities for the modes of the infrastructural components, representing our best estimates of the degree of compromise in each such piece of infrastructure. Following a session of diagnostic reasoning, these probabilities may be updated to the value of the *posterior* probabilities. Collectively these form a bi-partite Bayesian network; good algorithms [6] exist to compute posterior probabilities given observations.

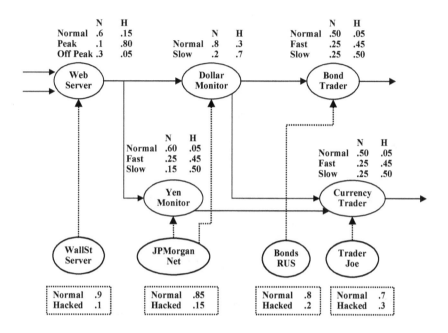

Figure 4: An Example of the Extended System Modeling Framework

E. Diagnostic Reasoning

Figure 4 shows an extended system model of a fictitious distributed financial system that we use to illustrate the reasoning process. The system consists of five interconnected software modules (Web-server, Dollar-Monitor, Bond-Trader, Yen-Monitor, Currency-Trader) utilizing four underlying computational resources (WallSt-Server, JPMorgan-Net, BondRUs, Trader-Joe). For each computational component we show the conditional probability tables that show how the behavioral modes of each computational resource probabilistically depend on the modes of the underlying resources (each resource has two modes, normal and hacked). Note that two computations (Dollar-Monitor and Yen-Monitor) are supported by a common resource (JPMorgan-net) and compromises to this underlying resource are likely to affect both computations. The failure modes of these two computations are no longer independent; this is indicated by the conditional probabilities connecting the behavior modes of the JPMorgan-net to those of both Dollar-Monitor and Yen-Monitor. The specific conditional probabilities supplied describe the degree of coupling. Finally we show the *a priori* probabilities for the modes of the underlying resources.

15

As in earlier techniques, diagnosis is initiated when a discrepancy is detected; in this case this means that the predicted production time of an output differs from those actually observed after an input has been presented. The goal of the diagnostic process is to infer as much as possible about where the computation failed (so that we may recover from the failure) and about what parts of the infrastructure may be compromised (so that we can avoid using them again until corrective action is taken). We are therefore looking for two things: the most likely explanation(s) of the observed discrepancies and updated probabilities for the modes of the infrastructural components. To do this we use techniques similar to [4]. We eventually want to identify all conflict sets, and we also want to conduct a best first search to find that set of modes for the computational components which is the most likely explanation for the observed discrepancy.

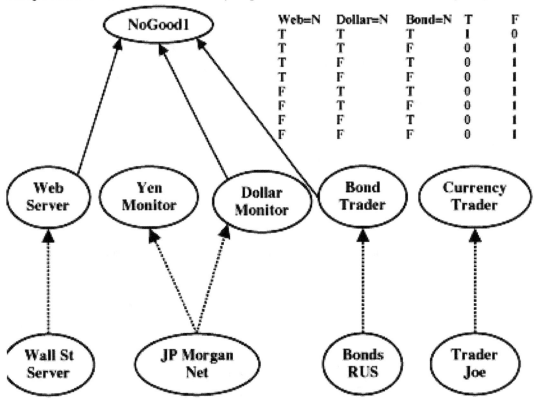

Figure 5: Adding a Conflict Node to the Bayesian Network

We do these tasks by a mixture of symbolic and Bayesian techniques; symbolic model-based reasoning is used to predict the behavior of the system, given an assumed set of behavioral modes. Whenever the symbolic reasoning process discovers a conflict (an incompatible set of behavioral modes), it incrementally extends the Bayesian network with a new node corresponding to the conflict (see below). Bayesian techniques are then used to solve the extended the extended network to get updated probabilities which are used to guide the search for the most likely diagnosis. Our behavioral models (the delay models) are used to predict behavior and compare the predictions with observations. When a discrepancy is detected, we use dependency tracing to find the conflict set underlying the discrepancy (i.e. a set of behavioral modes which are inconsistent).

At this point a new (binary truth value) node is added to the Bayesian network representing the conflict as shown in Figure 5. This node has an incoming arc from every node that participates in the conflict. It has a conditional probability table corresponding to a pure "logical and" i.e. its true state has a probability of 1.0 if all the incoming nodes are in their true states and it otherwise has probability 1.0 of being in its false state.

Since this node represents a logical contradiction, it is pinned in its false state. Adding this node to the network imposes a logical constraint on the probabilistic Bayesian network; the constraint imposed is that the conflict discovered by the symbolic, model-based behavioral simulation is impossible.

Once the "conflict" node is added to the Bayesian network and the network is solved, we obtain updated probabilities for each behavioral mode of each component. We can, therefore, examine the behavioral modes in the current conflict and pick that component whose current behavioral mode is least likely. We discard this mode, and pick the most likely alternative; we continue this process of detecting conflicts, discarding the least likely model in the conflict and picking its most likely alternative until a consistent set is found. This process is a very good heuristic for finding the most likely diagnosis (but it is just a heuristic).

Once the most likely diagnosis is found, we (optionally) continue to explore other combinations of behavioral modes, until possible minimal conflicts are discovered. Each of these conflicts extends the Bayesian network as before, but since we are (at this point) conducting an exhaustive search, we don't bother to solve the partially extended Bayesian network until we complete the enumeration.

At this point, we have found all the minimal conflicts and added conflict nodes to the Bayesian network for each. We therefore also know all the possible diagnoses since these are sets of behavioral modes (one for each component) that are not supersets of any conflict set. For each of these we create a node in the Bayesian network that is the logical-and of the nodes corresponding to the behavioral modes of the components. This node represents the probability of this particular diagnosis.

The Bayesian network is then solved one final time. This gives us updated probabilities for all possible diagnoses, for the behavioral modes of the computational components and for the modes of the underlying infrastructural components. Furthermore, these updated probabilities are those that are consistent with all the constraints we can obtain from the behavioral models. Thus, they represent as complete an assessment as is possible of the state of compromise in the infrastructure.

These posterior estimates can be taken as priors in further diagnostic tasks and they can also be used as a "trust model" informing users of the system (including self adaptive computations) of the trustworthiness of the various pieces of infrastructure which they will need to use.

17

F. Results

We show in Table 1, Table 2 and Table 3 the results of an analysis of the sample system are shown Figure 4. Inputs are supplied at times 10 and 15 for the two inputs of Web-Server and the outputs of Currency-Trader and Bond-Trader are observed at times 35 and 45 respectively[2].

Resource	Hacked Posterior	Hacked Prior	Normal Posterior	Normal Prior
Trader-Joe	.324	.300	.676	.700
Bonds R Us	.207	.200	.793	.800
JPMorgan-Net	.450	.150	.550	.850
WallSt-Server	.267	.100	.733	.900

Table 1: Posterior Probabilities of Resource Modes

There are more than a dozen possible diagnoses. It should be noted that the most likely diagnosis is actually not all that likely; in addition the next several diagnoses are nearly equally as likely. The most likely diagnosis is therefore not particularly informative for our two goals of recovering from the failure and steering away from compromised resources in the future. However, the posterior probabilities of the modes of the infrastructure components are, in fact, useful guides for the second of these goals. The posterior probabilities of the behavioral modes of the computational resources are useful guides for the first goal, because these probabilities aggregate the information contained in the individual diagnoses. The posterior probabilities of the modes of the underlying resources are shown in Table 1. The most significant change is the increase from .15 to .45 for the probability that the resource named JPMorgan-Net is hacked. Also the probability that Wallst-server was hacked increased from .1 to .267. In contrast, the probability that the other two resources are hacked doesn't change appreciably. This changes the trustworthiness ordering of the resources: JPMorgan-Net is *a posteriori* the least trustworthy resource, followed by Trader-Joe, while the *a priori* listing ranks Trader-Joe followed by Bonds-R-US as the least trustworthy. This follows from the fact that the JPMorgan-Net resources are utilized by the computations Yen-Monitor and Dollar-Monitor and are causing a common-mode failure.

---

[2] The implementation is in CommonLisp and uses the Joshua [7] rule-based reasoning system as well as the Ideal system [8] and in particular its implementation of the algorithm described in [6]. On a 300 MHz powerbook, the total solution time is under 1 minute. By far, the most expensive part of this is calculating the probabilities of the complete set of diagnoses. The most likely diagnosis and all conflict sets are located in less than 10 seconds

Computation	Mode	Probability
Web-Server	Off-Peak	.028
	Peak	541
	Normal	432
Dollar-Monitor	Slow	.738
	Normal	.262
Yen-Monitor	Slower	.516
	Slow	.339
	Normal	0.145
Bond-Trader	Slow	.590
	Fast	000
	Normal	.410
Currency-Trader	Slow	.612
	Fast	065
	Normal	0.323

Table 2: Posterior Probabilities of Computational Modes

G. Intermittent Faults

Intermittent faults are among the thorniest problems in diagnosis; to date, there has been little said in the literature about this issue. In hardware systems, intermittent faults often occur due to an actual failure coupled with random events (e.g. a loose wire which is randomly shaken into a position where it causes a short). In our context, intermittent faults occur because attackers are being careful about revealing their presence. To detect attacks, we would like it to be the case that faulty behavior greatly increases the likelihood that an infrastructural component is in a faulty mode while normal behavior should not greatly reduce a current belief that a component is faulty. But, if over long periods of time, no faulty behavior were observed, we would expect the probability that the component is faulty to decrease substantially.

Our current framework is capable of achieving exactly this behavior. Recall that the conditional probability links between the modes of infrastructure components and the modes of computational components is not necessarily one to one. In fact, the normal behavioral mode of a computational resource can have conditional probability links to both the normal and an abnormal mode of an infrastructure component, although the conditional probabilities on these links may have very different magnitudes. In fact, Figure 4 has just this structure: The normal mode of Yen-monitor, for example, is supported by both the Normal and Hacked modes of JPMorgan-Net with conditional probabilities of .6 and .05 respectively.

In this case, if the behavioral component is likely to be in its normal mode, this will tend to increase the posterior probabilities of both the normal and abnormal mode of the

19

infrastructure component. If the conditional probability linked to the abnormal mode is small (the typical case), then the posterior probability of the abnormal mode of the infrastructure component will increase only slightly, while its normal mode will increase more. On the other hand, if an abnormal mode of the computational resource has conditional probability links only to a single abnormal mode of the infrastructure component (again the typical case), then any manifestly abnormal behavior will increase the posterior probability of the abnormal mode of the infrastructure component. Continued normal behavior will cause this probability to decrease slowly.

Prob ability	Currency Trader	Bond Trader	Yen Monitor	Dollar Monitor	Web Server
.0898	Slow	Slow	Normal	Normal	Peak
.0876	Slow	Normal	Slow	Slow	Normal
.0855	Normal	Normal	slower	Slow	Normal
.0762	Slow	Normal	Really-Slow	Slow	Normal
.0641	Slow	Slow	Slow	Slow	Normal
.0626	Normal	Slow	Really-Slow	Slow	Normal
.0557	Slow	Slow	Really-Slow	Slow	Normal
.0468	Normal	Slow	Slow	Normal	Peak
.0416	Slow	Slow	Slow	Normal	Peak
.0321	Slow	Normal	Normal	Slow	Peak
.0306	Normal	Slow	slower	Normal	Peak
.0301	Normal	Normal	Slow	Slow	Peak
.0276	Slow	Slow	Slower	Slow	Off-Peak
.0272	Slow	Slow	Slower	Normal	Peak
.0268	Slow	Normal	Slow	Slow	Peak
.0262	Normal	Normal	Slower	Slow	Peak
.0260	Fast	Slow	Slower	Normal	Peak
.0235	Slow	Slow	Normal	Slow	Peak
.0233	Slow	Normal	Slower	Slow	Peak
.0223	Fast	Normal	Slower	Slow	Peak
.0221	Normal	Slow	Slow	Slow	Peak
.0196	Slow	Slow	Slow	Slow	Peak
.0192	Normal	Slow	Slower	Slow	Peak
.0171	Slow	Slow	Slower	Slow	Peak
.0163	Fast	Slow	Slower	Slow	Peak

Table 3: Posterior Probabilities of Diagnoses

VII. Conclusions and Future Work

A. Conclusions

The example above illustrates how model-based reasoning techniques can be used to extract information from a single run. Our example is intentionally fanciful since we are at the present concentrating on the development of the representational and reasoning frameworks. In future work we will explore realistic models of real systems. The information extracted is probabilistic and it sheds light both on the question of where the computation might have failed and on what underlying resources might have been compromised. It is notable that the identification of the most likely diagnosis is not particularly informative. For example, in the most likely diagnosis Yen-Monitor is in its Normal mode. However, the most likely behavioral mode for Yen-Monitor is its "Slower" mode, which occurs in many of the remaining diagnoses.

The posterior probabilities of the behavioral modes aggregate the probabilities from each of the possible diagnoses, producing an overall assessment that is more informative than any individual diagnosis. Of course, if there are few very few diagnoses, or the most likely diagnosis is extremely probable, then the probabilities of its behavioral modes will approximate the overall posterior probabilities.

If the first diagnosis discovered is found to have very high probability and if time is of the essence, then it can be used as a surrogate for the more thorough analysis. But, since the goal of the system is to recover from the failure and to steer away from future trouble, the production of individual diagnoses should not be the diagnostic focus. Instead, the goal of the diagnostic process should be to assess the overall probabilities of the behavioral modes of the computational and infrastructure components.

This is a different definition of the goal of diagnostic activity than has been used in previous research on model-based diagnosis. We have not yet addressed the details of how the system should use this information in forming a recovery plan. Nor have we yet addressed the question of what actions the system might take to obtain more information in future runs. The Minimum Entropy approach in [3] provides a useful framework. However, the current context provides more degrees of freedom; in addition to making new observations, we can also change the assignment of resources to computational components in a way that will maximize the expected gain in information. The details of this remain for future research.

B. A broader vision of the problem

We began this report with a scenario illustrating the need for a very broad attack on a number of problems relating to diagnosis, description, reconfiguration and resource management. However, only a limited portion, dealing with diagnosis, was actually funded and pursued within this project. Nevertheless, it has been impossible to pursue this agenda without thinking more deeply about how the diagnostic component would interact with other aspects of a future system. This section summarizes our thinking about these broader questions. We begin by summarizing the weaknesses we find in traditional approaches to secure computing.

1. The role of the trusted computing base

Traditional approaches to building survivable systems assume a framework of absolute trust. In this view, survivable systems require a provably impenetrable and incorruptible Trusted Computing Base (TCB). Unfortunately, we don't have TCB's, and experience suggests that we never will.

Instead, we will need to develop systems that can survive in an imperfect environment in which any resource may have been compromised to some extent. We believe that such systems can be built by restructuring the ways in which systems organize and perform computations. The central thrust of this approach is a radically different viewpoint of the trust relationships that a software system must bear to the computational resources it needs.

The traditional TCB-based approach takes a binary view of trust; computational resources either merit trust or not, and non-trusted resources should not be used. The traditional view also considers trustworthiness as a nearly static property of a resource: trust lost is never regained, short of major system reconstruction. Consequently, these systems wire decisions about how and where to perform computations into the code, making these decisions difficult to understand, and preventing the system from adapting to a changing runtime environment.

We agree with this viewpoint on the crucial role of the assessment and management of trust, but reject the assumptions about the binary, static nature of trust relationships as poor approximations to real-life computing situations. We instead base our approach on a different, more realistic set of assumptions:

- All computational resources must be considered suspect to some degree, but the degree of trust that should be accorded to a computational resource is not static, absolute, or known with full certainty. In particular, the degree of trustworthiness may change with further compromises or efforts at amelioration, in ways that can only be estimated on the basis of continuing experience. The system must thus continuously and actively monitor the computational environment at runtime to gather evidence about trustworthiness and to update its trust assessments.

- Exploiting assessments of trustworthiness requires structuring computations into layers of abstract services, with many distinct instantiations of each service. These specific instantiations of a service may vary in terms of the fidelity of the answers that they provide, the conditions under which they are appropriate, and the computational resources they require. But since the resources required by each possible instantiation have varying degrees of trustworthiness, each different way of rendering the service also has a specific risk associated with it.

- The best method for exploiting assessments of trustworthiness requires making explicit the information underlying decisions about how (and where) to perform a computation, and on formalizing this information and the method used to make the decision in a decision-theoretic framework. The overall system adapts to the dynamism of the environment and to the changing degrees of compromise in its components by deciding dynamically which approach to rendering a service provides the best likelihood of achieving the greatest benefit for the smallest risk. We do not require that the system uses explicit decision-theoretic calculations of maximal expected utility to make runtime decisions; the system may instead use the decision-theoretic formalizations to decide on policies and policy changes, which then are used to compile new code governing the relevant behaviors.

- The system must consider selected components to be fallible, even if it currently regards them as trustworthy, and must monitor its own and component behaviors to assure that the goals of computations are reached. In the event of a breakdown, the system must first update its assessments of the trustworthiness of the computational resources employed and then select an alternative approach to achieving the goal.

2. A New Set of Principles

These assumptions the lead us to adopt the following key principles:

- It is crucial to estimate to what degree and for what purposes a computer (or other computational resource) may be *trusted*, as this influences decisions about what tasks should be assigned to them, what contingencies should be provided for, and how much effort to spend watching over them.

- Making this estimate depends in turn on having a model of the possible ways in which a computational resource may be *compromised*.

- This in turn depends on having in place a system for long term *monitoring and analysis* of the computational infrastructure that can detect patterns of activity such as ``a period of attacks followed by quiescence followed by increasing degradation of service". Such a system must be capable of assimilating information from a variety of sources including both self-checking observation points within the application itself and *intrusion detection* systems.

- The application itself must be capable of *self-monitoring and diagnosis* and capable of *adaptation* so that it can best achieve its purposes with the available infrastructure.

- This, in turn, depends on the ability of the application, monitoring, and control systems to engage in rational decision-making about what resources they should use in order to achieve the best relation of expected benefit to risk.

Systems that can do the above things can be resilient in the face of concerted information attacks. They can carry on despite non-malicious intrusions; that is they can figure out when compromises that might be present within the infrastructure can't actually hurt them.

This viewpoint can be summarized in the following simple but revolutionary claim: ``Survivable systems make careful judgments about the trustworthiness of their computational environment and make rational resource allocation decisions accordingly."

The claim is deceptively simple: To make it real one needs to develop serious representations of the types of compromises, of the trustworthiness of a resource, and of the goals and purposes of the computational modules within an application. One also needs to build monitoring, analysis and trend detection tools and adaptive computational architectures. Finally, one needs to find a way to make the required rational decision making computationally tractable. The claim is also revolutionary: we note that with the single exception of the term *intrusion detection*, none of the key terms in our summary above are ordinarily talked about in the context of information survivability.

3. The Active Trust Management Architecture

These considerations motivate architecture both for the overall computational environment (Active Trust Management) and for the application systems that run within it (Autonomous Adaptive Survivable Systems). The environment as a whole must constantly collect and analyze data from a broad variety of sources, including the application systems, intrusion detection systems, system logs, network traffic analyzers, etc. The results of these analyses inform a ``Trust Model", a probabilistic representation of the trustworthiness of each computational resource in the environment. The application systems use this trust model to help decide which resources should be used to perform each major computational step; in particular, they try to choose that resource which will maximize the ratio of expected benefit to risk. This ``rational decision making" facility is provided as a standard utility within the environment. The application systems also monitor the execution of their own major components, checking that expected post-conditions are achieved. If these conditions fail to hold, diagnostic services are invoked to determine the most likely cause of the failures and thereby to determine the most promising way to recover. In addition to localizing the failure, the diagnostic services can also infer that underlying elements of the computational infrastructure are likely to have been compromised and these deductions are forwarded to the monitoring and analysis components of the environment to help inform its assessments of trustworthiness. Finally, having accumulated sufficient evidence, the monitoring and analysis systems may decide that it is likely that some resource has, in

24

fact, been compromised. This will have an immediate impact if the resource is being used to perform a computation which would be damaged by the specific form of compromise; in such cases, the monitoring and analysis components transmit ``alarms'' into the running application, causing it to abandon its work and to immediately initiate recovery efforts. Of course, a monitoring system which transmits such alarms too frequently is the computational equivalent of the shepherd boy who called ``wolf'' too often; the system again uses rational decision-making facilities to decide whether the circumstances warrant this choice.

Thus the application system forms a tight feedback control loop whose goal is to guarantee the best possible progress towards providing the services the application is intended to provide to its users (i.e., the applications are Autonomous Adaptive Survivable Systems ``AASS's''). The computational infrastructure also forms a feedback control loop whose goal is to maintain an accurate assessment of the trustworthiness of the computational resources; this assessment can then inform the application systems' decision making and self-monitoring which in turn helps inform the long-term assessments of trustworthiness (Active Trust Management ``ATM'').

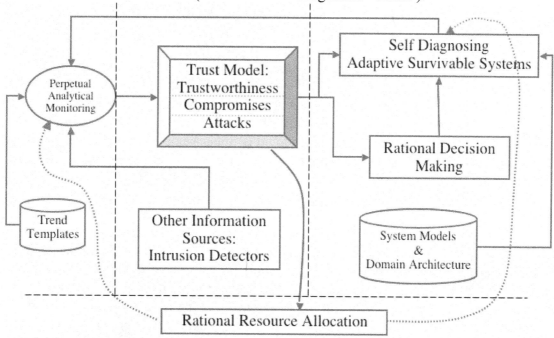

Figure 6: The Active Trust Management Architecture

This final section will briefly discuss the major components of such an architecture.

a) The Trust Model

Making rational decisions about how to use resources in an environment of imperfect trust requires information about what resources can be trusted, and for what purposes. It will be necessary to develop models of trust states that go beyond mere information about whether or how a system has been subject to attack to represent whether or how different properties of the system have been compromised, and finally to represent whether they can be trusted for a particular purpose even if compromised. It will also be necessary to represent the degree to which these judgments should be suspected or monitored. Trust assessments necessarily involve many dimensions along which a system can be trusted, since a system might be trusted for one operation (delivery of a message) but not for another (privacy of the message), and might be trusted with one type of information but not another (as in security classification systems). Formalizing trust-state models requires a language for making assertions about trust states, and reasoning about trust models requires effective methods for evaluating these statements.

These models provide the point of intersection among all the other elements of the approach. Indeed, trust plays a central role in resource allocation decisions. All decisions about what to do must be based on beliefs about the situation in which the action is to be taken. We can think of the degree of trust one places in a system as the degree to which one is willing to rely on the proper functioning of the system without also dedicating unusual effort to preparing for the contingency of failure. Since preparations for contingencies consume resources, this makes trust management a central resource allocation issue.

The trust model is organized into three levels above that of raw behavior:

The lowest level of the trust model represents the results of initial interpretations such as *attacks* and *anomalous behavior*. At this level we collect, filter and organize the necessary information so that it can trigger trend templates and feed into Bayesian inference networks. As we argued earlier, we are not primarily interested in what attacks or anomalous behaviors have taken place, but rather in what they imply about what compromises might actually be present.

The middle level of the trust model deals with *compromises*. The attack level only tells us that malicious or anomalous activity has taken place. But what we are interested in is whether someone has actually succeeded in an attack and has used that to exploit or corrupt resources. That such a compromise has been occurred can be inferred by matching the temporal patterns of activity to a trend template for a particular compromise. For example, the gaining of unauthorized user level access might be indicated by the temporal pattern of password sweeps followed by quiescence followed by increasing resource consumption.

The categorization of compromise states is relatively virgin territory, and one that requires new research. It would be natural to begin by first of all considering the properties that standard security techniques protect, such as the standard concepts of privacy, integrity, authentication, and non-repudiation. Within each of these dimensions, one can identify a variety of finer compromise types. For example, within the privacy dimension, one might distinguish knowledge of passwords from knowledge of the secrets these passwords protect, and from knowledge of the activity patterns of the authorized users of the secrets. One might distinguish visibility of these secrets to everyone from visibility to a narrower group. Within the integrity dimension, one can distinguish incompleteness from incorrectness.

A second dimension involves operational properties, essentially the different factors that make up quality of service. These properties include rate, timeliness (lack of delay), and evenness (freedom from jitter).

A third dimension involves command and control properties, such as the degree of confidence, the observability of security and operational properties, and the degree of controllability. This dimension is not covered by the first two sets. For example, loss of the ability to control the operational system might come about through a denial of service attack or other compromises of the control system, and loss of observability might come about through attacks on the monitoring system.

A fourth dimension distinguishes different subsystems, such as the intra-system communications network, the primary operational processes, the security mechanisms, or the monitoring subsystem. These distinctions may be made even more finely, to distinguish the types of information, operations, information sources or destinations affected, and the identity and roles of people participating in or affected by the compromises. (In this last situation, one possible compromise might be that someone inside is leaking passwords or other access information).

The highest level of the trust model deals with trustworthiness. The fact that a resource has been compromised does not in and of itself imply that it is totally unsafe to utilize it. That conclusion depends on the precise way in which the consumer wants to utilize the resource as well as on assessments of the *intention* of the compromiser. Consider two different attack scenarios: in the first, the system is compromised by ``teenaged hackers'' looking for free resources, in the second it is compromised by state-sponsored malicious agents. Clearly, we should generally be more wary of using a resource in the second case than the first; but if we are not very sensitive to quality of service and perhaps only care about the integrity of our data, then the first case is not all that risky.

Knowledge of attack types mainly guides the organization's attempts to defend against future attacks. Knowledge of compromises indicates the threats to operations. Knowledge of trust states guides how the organization carries on in the face of partially understood compromises. Because intent plays a central role, it too must be modeled throughout the three layers, moving from raw reports about behavior at the base level, to statements about intent in the middle layer and finally entering into assessments of trustworthiness at the highest level.

b) Perpetual Analytic Monitoring keeps the Trust Model current by detecting events and Trend Patterns which are indicative of compromise

Building a trust model involves more than just detecting an intrusion. Indeed, what is more important is a template of activity patterns consisting of several temporal regions:

In a typical takeover involving the theft of a user password we would expect to see the following activities: First there would be a period of attacks (particularly password scans). Then there would be a ``quiescent period''. Then there would be a period of increasing degradation of service. Finally, there would be a leveling off of the degradation but at the existing high level. We call such a temporal pattern a ``trend template''. In our previous work we have developed a representation language for trend templates and tools for online monitoring and analysis of data streams so as to recognize instances of trend templates in the stream.

The goal of Perpetual Analytic Monitoring is to assess the trustworthiness of the computational resources in the environment. This in turn requires us to make estimates of the likelihood that a resource has been compromised in a particular way. We believe that trend templates represent a necessary tool for doing so. Of course, the overall matching of trend templates depends on tools that can detect periods of uniform behavior (e.g., uniformly increasing, constant, oscillating at constant frequency).

Trend templates are necessary, but not sufficient in themselves. We also need to make inferences about the factual situation at hand (e.g., are international tensions rising?) and about the intentions, and states of mind of significant players (e.g., would it be likely that they are trying to attack me?). All of these inferences involve the combining of evidence to provide assessments of the likelihood of certain propositions. Bayesian networks provide a convenient formalism for representing and reasoning with basic probabilistic information.

Monitoring mechanisms must be capable of assimilating information from a broad variety of information sources including Intrusion Detection systems, self-monitoring by the application system, system logs, network traffic analyzers, etc The principal goal of Monitoring and Analysis tools is to keep the Trust Model current. However, when these tools have achieved a high degree of confidence that a compromise has occurred, the monitoring and analysis system must generate an alarm that may lead currently executing application components to rollback and attempt to use alternative strategies and resources. Deciding when to generate such an alarm is not trivial; if it is done too liberally then applications will never get useful work done as they service an endless stream of alarms. If it is done too conservatively, then application components will be corrupted. The decision to sound the alarm must be based on a decision theoretic analysis of the expected benefit and risks associated with raising an alarm.

c) The Autonomous Adaptive Survivable System infrastructure uses Trust Models and models of the purpose of expected behavior to select computational strategy and to detect and recover from compromises

Autonomous Adaptive Survivable Systems have the goal of adapting to the variations in their environment so as to render useful services under all conditions. In the context of Intrusion Tolerance, this means that useful services must be provided even when there have been successful information attacks.

AASS's achieve adaptivity in two ways: First, they include many alternative implementations of the major computational steps, each of which achieves the same goal but in different ways. Before each step is actually initiated, the system first assesses which of these most appropriate in light of what is known about the environment. In the Survivability context, such decisions must be rational decisions rooted in the Trust Model.

The second way in which the system achieves adaptivity is by noticing when its components fail to achieve the conditions relied on by other modules, initiating diagnostic, rollback and recovery services. This depends on effective monitoring of system performance and trustworthiness that in turn requires a structured view of the system as decomposed into modules, together with teleological annotations that identify prerequisites, post-conditions and invariant conditions of the modules. These teleological models also include links describing how the post-conditions of the modules interact to achieve the goals of the main system and the prerequisites of modules further downstream.

The model-based diagnostic services we described earlier will play a key role in an AASS's ability to recover from a failure. The diagnosis helps the application decide how to recover from the failure and restore normal functioning. It also provides evidence to the overall monitoring environment about the trustworthiness of the underlying computational resources, particularly when the most likely diagnoses indicate that one of the resources has been compromised.

d) Rational Decision Making uses decision-theoretic models and the Trust Model to control decisions about component selection and resource allocation

We assess system trustworthiness and performance according to the trust and teleological models in order to make decisions about how to allocate computational resources. To ensure that these decisions represent a good basis for system operation, we will develop detailed decision-theoretic models of trustworthiness, suspicion, and related concepts as applied to information systems and their components. These models will relate notions such as attractiveness of a system as a target, likelihood of being attacked, likelihood of being compromised by an attack, riskiness of use of the system, importance or criticality of the system for different purposes, etc.

The models will also relate estimates of system properties to an adaptive system of decision-theoretic preferences that express the values guiding the operation of both system modules and the system as a whole. We will develop mechanisms that use these elements to allocate system resources optimally given task demands, trustworthiness judgments, and the resources available.

VIII. Project Outreach

A. Cumulative Chronological List of Written Publications

Shrobe, Howard: "Model-based Troubleshooting for Information Survivability"
Proceedings of DISCEX I, Hilton Head, 1998.

Shrobe, Howard and Doyle, John, "Active Trust Management for Adaptive Survivable
Systems" First International Workshop on Self-Adaptive Systems, 1999.

B. Cumulative List of Professional Personnel Associated with the Research Effort

Dr. Howard E. Shrobe
Dr. John Doyle
Professor Randall Davis
John Mallery
Erwin Tam

C. Cumulative List of Papers Presented at Meetings

Howard Shrobe, "Information Survivability" EECS Departmental Colloquium, MIT, 1998.

Howard Shrobe, "Information Survivability" Oakland Security Conference, 1998.

Howard Shrobe, Invited Keynote Address, The Innovative Applications of AI Conference
(part of the AAAI National Conference), August 1999.

Shrobe, Howard: "Model-based Troubleshooting for Information Survivability"
Proceedings of DISCEX I, Hilton Head, 1998.

Shrobe, Howard and Doyle, John, "Active Trust Management for Adaptive Survivable
Systems" First International Workshop on Self-Adaptive Systems, 1999.

D. Consultative and Advisory Functions to Other Laboratories

Dr. Howard Shrobe presented a talk at a PI Meeting of the Global Mobile Computing
Program (GLOMO) at Lincoln Labs, outlining the ideas of Information Survivability as
Adaptive Computing and also explaining Active Networking research ideas.

E. Theses related to the research

Erwin Tam, Integration of a Bayesian Net Solver with the KBCW Comlink System
and a Network Intrusion Diagnosis System, August 27, 1999.

Bibliography

1. Davis, R., and Shrobe, H 1982. "Diagnosis based on structure and function." In **Proceedings of the AAAI National Conference on Artificial Intelligence**, 137--142. AAAI.

2. Davis, R 1984. "Diagnostic reasoning based on structure and behavior." **Artificial Intelligence** 24:347--410.

3. deKleer, J., and Williams, B. 1987. "Diagnosing multiple faults". **Artificial Intelligence** 32(1):97--130.

4. deKleer, J., and Williams, B. 1989. "Diagnosis with behavior modes. In Proceedings of the International Joint Conference on Artificial Intelligence.

5. Hamscher, W., and Davis, R. 1988. " Model-based reasoning: Troubleshooting." In Shrobe, H., and ed., **Exploring Artificial Intelligence**}. AAAI. 297--346.

6. Jensen, F.; Lauritzen, S.; and Olesen, K. 1989. "Bayesian updating in recursive graphical models by local computations." **Technical Report R 89-15**, University of Aalborg, Institute for Electronic Systems, Department of Mathematics and Computer Science.

7. Rowley, S.; Shrobe, H.; Cassels, R.; and Hamscher, W. 1987. "Joshua: Uniform access to heterogeneous knowledge structures (or why joshing is better than conniving or planning". In National **Conference on Artificial Intelligence**, 48--52. AAAI.

8. Srinivas, S., and Breese, J. 1989. "Ideal: Influence diagram evaluation and analysis in lisp, documentation and users guide." **Technical Report~23**, Rockwell International Science Center, Palo Alto Laboratory, Palo Alto, CA.

www.ingramcontent.com/pod-product-compliance
Lightning Source LLC
Chambersburg PA
CBHW060514060326

40689CB00020B/4736